# Inspirational Home Decor Book: Transform Your Living Space with Style

Serene Art Press

2024

*Image Sources and Disclaimer*

*The images in this book are sourced from iStockphoto, Ideogram, and various open sources, with appropriate attributions included directly on the photos. The primary goal of this book is to provide style models and guide readers through different design styles, rather than presenting exact, real-life homes and designs. While every effort has been made to ensure the accuracy and quality of the images, the author does not assume responsibility for any errors or discrepancies. This book is intended for inspirational purposes, and the depicted designs are meant to illustrate general concepts rather than serve as exact representations.*

# EDITORIAL

Welcome to "Inspirational Home Decor Book: Transform Your Living Space with Style". This book is designed to be your comprehensive guide to creating a beautiful and functional home that reflects your unique taste and lifestyle. Whether you're planning a complete renovation or simply looking to refresh your current decor, you'll find inspiration and practical advice within these pages.

Our goal is to help you navigate the world of home decor with confidence. We've covered a wide range of styles, from the sleek lines of Modern design to the cozy charm of Rustic decor, ensuring there's something for everyone. Each chapter provides an in-depth look at the characteristics, key elements, and inspirational examples of each style, helping you to make informed decisions that suit your home and your needs.

As you explore the different styles, remember that decorating your home is a personal journey. It's about creating a space where you and your family feel comfortable, happy, and inspired. We hope this book provides you with the tools and ideas to transform your living space into a place you'll love to call home.

Thank you for choosing "Inspirational Home Decor Book". Let's embark on this journey together to create a home that is both beautiful and functional.

*Serene Art Press*

# Content

20.

### Chapter 1: Modern Style /04

Explore the origins and evolution of modern home decor, highlighting key figures and trends. Discover essential elements like clean-lined furniture, statement lighting, and open floor plans, and get inspired by practical examples for modern living spaces.

### Chapter 2: Classic Style /28

Trace the roots of classic decor from European influences to its modern adaptations. Understand the importance of antique furniture, ornate designs, and high-quality materials in creating a timeless and elegant aesthetic.

41.

### Chapter 3: Scandinavian Style /50

Learn about the origins and evolution of Scandinavian decor, emphasizing simplicity, functionality, and a connection to nature. Explore key elements like functional furniture, natural light, and sustainable materials, with practical examples for cozy and functional spaces.

75.

### Chapter 4: Bohemian Style /72

Delve into the artistic and nomadic origins of Bohemian decor, evolving into a modern eclectic style with vibrant colors and mixed patterns. Mix vintage furniture, ambient lighting, and natural materials to create personalized and artistic spaces.

### Chapter 5: Industrial Style /98

Explore the utilitarian origins of industrial decor, evolving into stylish homes with exposed structures and raw materials. Learn about reclaimed furniture, industrial lighting, and materials like concrete and steel to create raw and chic designs.

136.

### Chapter 6: Minimalist Style /120

Explore the origins and evolution of modern home decor, highlighting key figures and trends. Understand how neutral palettes and industTrace the evolution of minimalist decor from modernist movements to contemporary clean lines, emphasizing simplicity and functionality.

### Chapter 7: Rustic Style /142

Discover the origins of rustic decor in countryside homes, evolving into modern interpretations with natural materials and a cozy atmosphere. Learn about wooden furniture, warm lighting, and earthy palettes to create warm and inviting spaces.

172.

### Chapter 8: Coastal Style /168

Understand the evolution of coastal decor from seaside homes to modern beachy vibes, emphasizing light, airy, and relaxed atmospheres. Discover light, comfortable furniture, natural light, and soft blues and whites for breezy designs.

239.

### Chapter 9: Retro Style /194

Explore the origins of retro decor in mid-20th century design, evolving into modern interpretations with bold, bright, and cheerful hues. Learn about iconic furniture, statement lighting, and dynamic color palettes for vibrant and nostalgic designs.

### Chapter 10: Eclectic Style /220

Understand the origins and evolution of eclectic decor, highlighting bold and diverse color schemes and a mix of styles. Explore mismatched furniture, statement lighting, and personalized decor reflecting individual style for creative and vibrant spaces.

INSPIRATIONAL HOME DECOR

# The Importance of Choosing the Right Home Decor Style

Selecting the right home decor style is a crucial step in creating a living space that is not only visually appealing but also functional and comfortable. The decor style you choose reflects your personality, lifestyle, and preferences, making your home a true reflection of who you are. Here are several reasons why choosing the right decor style is so important:

**Personal Expression**
Your home is an extension of yourself, and its decor should reflect your unique personality and tastes. A well-chosen decor style can communicate your individuality and make your home a place where you feel truly at ease. Whether you prefer the sleek lines of modern design, the cozy charm of rustic decor, or the vibrant energy of bohemian style, your home should be a space that feels authentically you.

**Functional Living**
Different decor styles offer various functional benefits that can enhance your daily living experience. For example, a minimalist style promotes a clutter-free environment, which can reduce stress and increase productivity. On the other hand, a transitional style blends traditional and contemporary elements, providing both comfort and modern conveniences. By choosing a style that aligns with your lifestyle, you can create a home that works for you on a practical level.

**Aesthetic Appeal**
The visual impact of a well-decorated home cannot be overstated. A cohesive decor style brings a sense of harmony and balance to your space, making it more pleasant to live in and more inviting for guests. Consistency in style helps avoid a disjointed appearance and ensures that all elements of your decor complement each other, creating a unified look.

## Resale Value

If you plan to sell your home in the future, the right decor style can significantly enhance its marketability. Homes with well-executed, popular decor styles tend to attract more buyers and can command higher prices. Neutral and widely appealing styles like modern, transitional, or Scandinavian often have broad market appeal and can make your home more attractive to potential buyers.

## Emotional Well-Being

Your home environment has a profound impact on your emotional well-being. A space that reflects your personal style and meets your functional needs can promote relaxation, happiness, and a sense of contentment. Conversely, a mismatched or poorly planned decor can lead to feelings of dissatisfaction and stress. By thoughtfully choosing a decor style, you can create a sanctuary that supports your mental and emotional health.

## Adaptability and Flexibility

Choosing a decor style that is adaptable can make it easier to update your home over time. Some styles, like eclectic or transitional, allow for greater flexibility in incorporating new trends and personal touches. This adaptability ensures that your home can evolve with your changing tastes and needs without requiring a complete overhaul.

Selecting the right home decor style is an investment in your happiness and quality of life. It allows you to create a space that is not only beautiful but also functional, comfortable, and reflective of your unique personality. By understanding the importance of decor and thoughtfully choosing a style that suits you, you can transform your living space into a true home.

INSPIRATIONAL HOME DECOR

# Chapter 1: Modern Style

INSPIRATIONAL HOME DECOR

# *The Art of Modern Simplicity*

The modernist movement, which began in the early 20th century, was a response to the ornate and overly decorative styles of the Victorian era. It embraced simplicity, functionality, and the honest use of materials. The movement was deeply influenced by the industrial revolution, which introduced new materials and techniques that shaped modern architecture and design.

One of the most influential figures of this movement was *Le Corbusier*, a Swiss-French architect whose work emphasized functionality and simplicity. He introduced the concept of the house as a "machine for living," promoting open floor plans, minimalistic aesthetics, and the use of modern materials like concrete and steel. One of his most famous works, Villa Savoye, exemplifies these principles with its clean lines and functional design.

*Ludwig Mies van der Rohe*, a German-American architect, is known for his maxim "less is more." His designs are characterized by an open floor plan and the use of modern materials such as glass and steel. The Farnsworth House, one of his iconic projects, showcases his approach to minimalism and his belief in the importance of space and light.

*Walter Gropius*, the founder of the Bauhaus School in Germany, played a crucial role in the development of modernist design. The Bauhaus philosophy integrated art, craft, and technology, promoting the idea that design should be functional, beautiful, and accessible to all. The Bauhaus Dessau, designed by Gropius, is a landmark of modern architecture, embodying the principles of functionalism and simplicity.

Le Corbusier
Photo by Erling Mandelmann, via Wikimedia Commons.

INSPIRATIONAL HOME DECOR

The mid-century modern movement, which spanned roughly from the 1940s to the 1960s, built upon the principles established by early modernists. This era was characterized by clean lines, organic curves, and a love for new materials like plastic, plywood, and aluminum. Functional furniture with sleek lines, the integration of indoor and outdoor spaces, and an emphasis on simplicity and utility defined this style. Designers like *Charles and Ray Eames* and *Eero Saarinen* were pivotal in shaping mid-century modern design.

The movement also emphasized the connection between indoor and outdoor spaces, a concept championed by architects like *Richard Neutra* and *Eero Saarinen*. Neutra's Kaufmann House in Palm Springs and Saarinen's Tulip Chair are iconic examples of how mid-century modern design blended functionality with organic forms and natural materials.

Following the mid-century period, modern design continued to evolve, incorporating advancements in technology and changing aesthetic preferences. The minimalist movement, which gained prominence in the 1980s and 1990s, further stripped down design to its essentials, focusing on clean, uncluttered spaces. Influential designers like *John Pawson* and *Tadao Ando* embraced minimalism, using simple forms and natural light to create serene environments.

In the 21st century, contemporary interpretations of modern decor have incorporated elements of warmth and comfort. There is a greater emphasis on sustainability and eco-friendly design practices, with designers using recycled materials and energy-efficient technologies. The integration of smart home systems has also become a hallmark of contemporary modern decor, seamlessly blending technology with minimalist aesthetics. By understanding the historical roots and evolution of modern home decor, we can appreciate its enduring appeal and relevance in today's design landscape.

View of the Kaufman House from the pool deck

# Key Elements of Modern Home Decor

### Furniture:
Clean lines, geometric shapes, multi-functional pieces

Modern furniture is defined by its simplicity and functionality. It often features clean lines and geometric shapes, which contribute to a minimalist aesthetic. Multi-functional pieces are highly valued for their practicality in maximizing space, especially in smaller living areas. For example, a sofa with hidden storage or a convertible coffee table that doubles as a workspace.

INSPIRATIONAL HOME DECOR

## Lighting:
### Maximizing natural light, statement lighting fixtures

Lighting plays a crucial role in modern home decor, with an emphasis on maximizing natural light. Large, unobstructed windows and skylights are common features. When natural light isn't sufficient, modern decor incorporates statement lighting fixtures that serve both a functional and aesthetic purpose. Think sleek floor lamps, pendant lights, and recessed lighting that highlights architectural elements.

## Materials:
### Industrial materials, natural elements

Modern decor often blends industrial materials such as steel, glass, and concrete with natural elements like wood and stone. This combination creates a balance between the raw, edgy feel of industrial design and the warmth of natural textures. For example, a living room might feature a concrete floor with a wooden coffee table and metal-framed sofas.

## Color Scheme:
### Dominance of neutral palettes with bold accents

A neutral color palette is a hallmark of modern decor, creating a calm and cohesive backdrop. Shades of white, gray, black, and beige dominate. However, bold accents are strategically used to add interest and personality to the space. This can be achieved through colorful throw pillows, vibrant art pieces, or a striking piece of furniture.

INSPIRATIONAL HOME DECOR

## Technology:
### Integrated smart systems

Modern homes seamlessly integrate technology to enhance convenience and efficiency. Smart home systems control lighting, heating, and security, often through voice commands or mobile apps. Hidden wiring, built-in speakers, and smart appliances that blend into the decor are typical features. The goal is to create a space that is both functional and aesthetically pleasing.

INSPIRATIONAL HOME DECOR

**Accessories:**
Bold art pieces, minimalist decor items

While modern decor leans towards minimalism, it doesn't shy away from bold accessories that make a statement. Art pieces, whether a large abstract painting or a series of black-and-white photographs, are chosen for their impact. Decor items are kept minimal and purposeful, such as a single sculptural vase or a unique clock, to avoid visual clutter.

INSPIRATIONAL HOME DECOR

INSPIRATIONAL HOME DECOR

INSPIRATIONAL HOME DECOR

## Open Spaces:
### Design open floor plans to enhance space

Open floor plans are a key element of modern home design, promoting a sense of spaciousness and fluidity. This design approach removes barriers between common areas, such as the kitchen, dining, and living rooms, creating a more social and interactive environment. Furniture arrangement and area rugs are used to define different zones within the open space.

INSPIRATIONAL HOME DECOR

The importance of open floor plans extends beyond aesthetics; they enhance the functionality of the home by providing flexible spaces that can adapt to different needs and activities. This concept encourages a more connected and dynamic living environment, where family members and guests can interact more freely, making the home feel more inviting and cohesive.

**Textures:**
Mixing textures to add depth and interest

Incorporating a variety of textures is essential to prevent modern spaces from feeling cold or sterile. A mix of textures, such as a plush wool rug, a smooth leather sofa, a rough concrete wall, and a sleek glass coffee table, adds depth and interest. Textures can be introduced through textiles, finishes, and materials, creating a layered and inviting atmosphere.

INSPIRATIONAL HOME DECOR

# Modern Decor Examples and Inspiration

INSPIRATIONAL HOME DECOR

INSPIRATIONAL HOME DECOR

INSPIRATIONAL HOME DECOR

INSPIRATIONAL HOME DECOR

INSPIRATIONAL HOME DECOR

INSPIRATIONAL HOME DECOR

"Luxury is when it seems flawless, when you reach the right balance between all elements. Understated theatricality – that is what my luxury is all about."
Jean-Louis Deniot

INSPIRATIONAL HOME DECOR

# Chapter 2: Classic Style

INSPIRATIONAL HOME DECOR

# The Elegance of Classic Home Decor

Classic home decor has its roots in the grand European styles of the 17th, 18th, and 19th centuries, drawing inspiration from the opulent interiors of the French, English, and Italian aristocracy.

This style emphasizes symmetry, balance, and proportion, reflecting the ideals of order and harmony. Key influences include the elaborate ornamentation of the Baroque period, the refined elegance of the Rococo era, and the neoclassical elements of the late 18th century.

The French influence is particularly strong, with the lavishness of the Louis XIV, XV, and XVI periods setting a high standard for luxury and refinement. French classic decor is characterized by gilded mirrors, ornate moldings, crystal chandeliers, and luxurious fabrics like silk and velvet.

In England, the Georgian and Regency periods contributed significantly to classic decor. These styles emphasize elegant simplicity and understated luxury, featuring mahogany furniture, detailed plasterwork, and richly colored textiles.

Italian classic decor, particularly from the Renaissance and Baroque periods, is known for its grandeur and use of rich materials like marble and gold leaf. This influence is evident in the grandiose architectural details, such as coffered ceilings and intricate frescoes.

Bruhl, Germany, September 17, 2023: Augustusburg and Falkenlust Palaces historical building complex in Bruhl Germany

# Evolution: Transition from Traditional to Modern Classic Styles

While traditional classic decor remains popular for its timeless elegance, it has also evolved to meet contemporary tastes, resulting in what is known as modern classic or transitional style. This modern interpretation retains the sophisticated elements of classic decor but incorporates a more streamlined and functional approach.

*Streamlined Furniture:* Modern classic decor often features simplified versions of traditional furniture. While the pieces maintain their elegant shapes and luxurious materials, they are less ornate and more practical for modern living.

*Neutral Color Palettes:* Unlike the rich, bold colors of traditional classic decor, modern classic interiors often use a more subdued, neutral color palette. Whites, grays, and soft beiges are commonly used to create a serene and sophisticated environment, while still allowing for the inclusion of luxurious textures and finishes.

*Blending Old and New:* One of the defining features of modern classic style is the seamless blending of old and new elements. Antique furniture and decor items are often paired with contemporary pieces, creating a balanced and harmonious look. For example, a traditional crystal chandelier might hang above a modern glass dining table, or a classic wingback chair might be upholstered in a contemporary fabric.

*Functional Spaces*: Modern classic interiors are designed to be not only beautiful but also functional. Open floor plans, built-in storage solutions, and modern amenities are incorporated into the design, making the space practical for everyday living while still retaining its classic elegance.

By understanding the historical roots and the evolution of classic home decor, we can appreciate how this timeless style has adapted to contemporary needs while preserving its core principles of elegance and sophistication.

# Key Elements of Classic Home Decor

## Furniture:
Antique Pieces, Ornate Designs, High-Quality Materials

Classic home decor is characterized by its use of antique furniture that embodies elegance and craftsmanship. These pieces often feature intricate carvings, ornate details, and are made from high-quality materials like solid wood and rich fabrics. Iconic examples include the claw-footed tables, roll-arm sofas, and elaborate armoires. The furniture pieces are typically sturdy and built to last, often passed down through generations as family heirlooms. In modern classic decor, these antiques are sometimes paired with contemporary pieces to create a balanced and timeless look.

INSPIRATIONAL HOME DECOR

## Lighting:
## Chandeliers, Traditional Sconces, Warm Lighting

Lighting in classic decor is both functional and decorative. Chandeliers, often featuring crystal or ornate metalwork, serve as focal points in rooms like dining areas and grand foyers. Traditional wall sconces provide ambient lighting and add to the room's aesthetic. Warm lighting, achieved through the use of incandescent bulbs and carefully chosen lampshades, enhances the inviting and luxurious atmosphere typical of classic interiors.

INSPIRATIONAL HOME DECOR

INSPIRATIONAL HOME DECOR

**Materials:**
Wood, Marble, Rich Fabrics

The use of high-quality materials is a hallmark of classic home decor. Wood is a primary material, often dark-stained or painted in rich hues, and used in furniture, paneling, and flooring. Marble is frequently used for fireplaces, countertops, and flooring, adding a sense of grandeur and permanence. Rich fabrics like velvet, silk, and brocade are used for upholstery, drapery, and accessories, contributing to the opulent feel of the space.

INSPIRATIONAL HOME DECOR

**Color Scheme:**
Warm, Rich Palettes

Classic interiors typically feature warm and rich color palettes that create a cozy and inviting environment. Common colors include deep reds, golds, greens, and browns, which are often complemented by neutral tones like cream and beige. These colors are used to highlight architectural details and furnishings, ensuring a cohesive and luxurious look throughout the home.

"The Birth of Venus" by Sandro Botticelli

INSPIRATIONAL HOME DECOR

INSPIRATIONAL HOME DECOR

### Accessories:
### Classic Art, Sculptures, Elegant Decor Items

Accessories in classic home decor are carefully selected to enhance the overall theme of elegance and sophistication. Classic art, such as oil paintings in gilded frames, and sculptures are prominently displayed. Decor items include ornate mirrors, vases, and clocks, all chosen for their aesthetic appeal and historical significance. These accessories not only add visual interest but also reflect the homeowner's taste and appreciation for fine art.

**Detailing:**
Ornate Moldings and Carvings

Ornate moldings and carvings are defining features of classic home decor. Crown moldings, wainscoting, and chair rails add architectural interest and elegance to walls and ceilings. Furniture pieces often include detailed carvings, such as floral motifs and scrollwork, showcasing the craftsmanship involved. These details are meticulously designed and executed, adding to the overall sense of refinement and historical continuity in the decor.

# Classic Decor Examples

INSPIRATIONAL HOME DECOR

## *and Inspiration*

INSPIRATIONAL HOME DECOR

INSPIRATIONAL HOME DECOR

INSPIRATIONAL HOME DECOR

"Be faithful to your own taste, because nothing you really like is ever out of style."
**Billy Baldwin**

INSPIRATIONAL HOME DECOR

# Chapter 3: Scandinavian Style

# The Simplicity of Scandinavian Home Decor

Scandinavian home decor has its roots deeply embedded in the cultural and geographical context of the Nordic countries, including Denmark, Sweden, Norway, and Finland. The harsh, long winters and the need for a functional yet cozy living environment heavily influenced the development of this design style. Scandinavian decor emphasizes simplicity, minimalism, and functionality, reflecting the region's appreciation for nature and the need to maximize light in the darker months.

Historically, Scandinavian interiors were characterized by their use of natural materials such as wood, wool, and leather, which provided both warmth and durability. The traditional color palette was dominated by whites and light neutrals, helping to brighten interior spaces during the long, dark winters. Additionally, craftsmanship and quality were highly valued, resulting in furniture and decor that were built to last.

Over time, Scandinavian decor has evolved while maintaining its core principles of simplicity and functionality. The mid-20th century brought international recognition to Scandinavian design, largely due to the influence of designers like *Arne Jacobsen, Alvar Aalto*, and *Hans Wegner*. Their work emphasized clean lines, organic forms, and the use of innovative materials, further shaping the modern interpretation of Scandinavian style.

The concept of "hygge," a Danish term that encompasses coziness, comfort, and a sense of well-being, has become central to contemporary Scandinavian decor. Modern Scandinavian interiors focus on creating inviting and relaxed spaces that promote a sense of tranquility and warmth. This is achieved through the use of soft textiles, warm lighting, and natural elements, alongside the traditional emphasis on functionality and simplicity.

Today, Scandinavian design continues to be celebrated for its timeless appeal and adaptability. It effortlessly combines traditional elements with modern aesthetics, making it a popular choice for creating serene and stylish homes that prioritize comfort and practicality.

By understanding the historical roots and evolution of Scandinavian home decor, we can appreciate its enduring influence and relevance in creating spaces that are both beautiful and functional.

## Furniture:
### Functional, Minimalistic Designs, Natural Materials

Scandinavian furniture is characterized by its functional and minimalist design. Pieces are typically simple yet elegant, focusing on clean lines and practical uses. Furniture often incorporates natural materials such as light woods (like pine and birch), which are sustainably sourced. Iconic pieces like the Eames chair or the sleek lines of IKEA furniture exemplify this style, blending form with function.

INSPIRATIONAL HOME DECOR

## Lighting:
### Maximizing Natural Light, Simple Fixtures

Lighting is a crucial element in Scandinavian decor due to the long, dark winters in Nordic countries. Interiors are designed to maximize natural light, often featuring large, unobstructed windows. When natural light is insufficient, simple and understated fixtures are used to illuminate spaces. Pendant lights, wall sconces, and floor lamps with clean, modern designs are common, often in white or metallic finishes to reflect light.

INSPIRATIONAL HOME DECOR

## Materials:
### Wood, Natural Fibers, Sustainable Materials

The use of natural materials is a hallmark of Scandinavian design. Light woods such as pine, birch, and oak are prevalent in flooring, furniture, and accessories. Natural fibers like wool, linen, and cotton are commonly used for textiles, contributing to a cozy and inviting atmosphere.

Sustainability is also a key consideration, with many designers prioritizing eco-friendly materials and practices.

INSPIRATIONAL HOME DECOR

**Color Scheme:**
Light and Airy Palettes

Scandinavian interiors typically feature light and airy color palettes to enhance the sense of space and brightness. White is the dominant color, often complemented by soft grays, muted blues, and earthy tones. This neutral palette helps to reflect light and create a serene and uncluttered environment. Occasionally, pops of color are introduced through accessories or textiles to add visual interest.

INSPIRATIONAL HOME DECOR

INSPIRATIONAL HOME DECOR

## Patterns:
### Subtle Patterns Inspired by Nature

Patterns in Scandinavian design are typically subtle and inspired by nature. Geometric shapes, botanical motifs, and simple stripes are common. These patterns are often found in textiles, wallpaper, and ceramics, adding a touch of character without overwhelming the space. The key is to keep patterns understated and harmonious with the overall color scheme.

## Indoor Plants:
### Bringing Nature Indoors

Incorporating indoor plants is a significant aspect of Scandinavian decor, reflecting the region's deep connection with nature. Plants like succulents, ferns, and potted trees bring life and color to interiors, improving air quality and adding a refreshing natural element. Simple, unadorned pots and planters are used to maintain the minimalist aesthetic.

INSPIRATIONAL HOME DECOR

# Scandinavian Decor Examples and Inspiration

INSPIRATIONAL HOME DECOR

INSPIRATIONAL HOME DECOR

INSPIRATIONAL HOME DECOR

INSPIRATIONAL HOME DECOR

INSPIRATIONAL HOME DECOR

INSPIRATIONAL HOME DECOR

INSPIRATIONAL HOME DECOR

INSPIRATIONAL HOME DECOR

"The details are not the details. They make the design."
**Charles Eames**

INSPIRATIONAL HOME DECOR

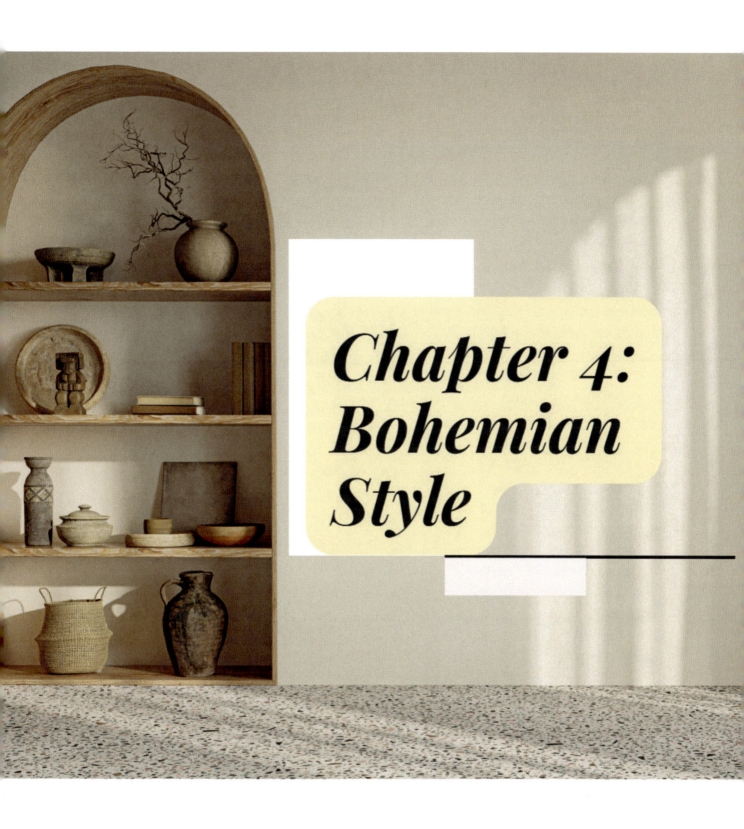

# Chapter 4: Bohemian Style

INSPIRATIONAL HOME DECOR

# The Eclectic Charm of Bohemian Home Decor

Bohemian home decor, often referred to as "Boho," has its roots in the free-spirited and artistic lifestyles of 19th-century Parisian artists, writers, and intellectuals. These individuals rejected the rigid norms of society and embraced a life of creativity, unconventionality, and a deep appreciation for beauty and art. The term "Bohemian" originally referred to the Romani people, mistakenly believed to have come from the Bohemia region in the Czech Republic. This style was later adopted by artists and creatives who valued a nomadic and unorthodox way of living.

INSPIRATIONAL HOME DECOR

The Bohemian style reflects a love for art, culture, and travel, often incorporating a mix of influences from around the world. It is characterized by a vibrant and eclectic mix of patterns, colors, and textures, creating a space that feels collected and curated over time. Key elements include richly patterned textiles, vintage and antique furniture, and a variety of accessories and artifacts that tell a story.

INSPIRATIONAL HOME DECOR

## From Traditional Bohemian to Modern Eclectic

While traditional Bohemian decor was heavily influenced by the lifestyles of 19th-century artists and nomads, it has evolved significantly over the years. The modern interpretation of Boho style, often referred to as "Modern Eclectic," retains the core elements of creativity and eclecticism but incorporates contemporary sensibilities and design principles.

Modern Boho decor often features a more curated and cohesive look, balancing the vibrant and eclectic elements with a more minimalist and intentional approach. The color palette, while still rich and diverse, often includes more muted and earthy tones, creating a harmonious and calming environment. Furniture and decor items are carefully chosen for their aesthetic and functional qualities, blending vintage pieces with modern accents.

The influence of global cultures remains a key component of modern Boho decor, with elements from various traditions and regions seamlessly integrated into the design. This includes the use of Moroccan rugs, Indian tapestries, African baskets, and Asian ceramics, among others. The result is a space that feels both worldly and personal, reflecting the homeowner's unique tastes and experiences.

In summary, Bohemian home decor has evolved from its artistic and nomadic origins to embrace a more modern and eclectic approach. It continues to celebrate individuality, creativity, and a love for art and culture, making it a timeless and versatile style that can be adapted to suit a variety of tastes and preferences.

# Key Elements of Bohemian Home Decor

**Furniture:**
Mismatched, Vintage Pieces, Low Seating

Bohemian home decor embraces an eclectic mix of furniture styles, with a preference for mismatched and vintage pieces. This can include anything from a well-worn leather sofa to a beautifully carved wooden coffee table. The focus is on creating a space that feels collected and curated over time, rather than designed all at once. Low seating options like floor cushions, poufs, and daybeds are also common, adding to the relaxed and inviting atmosphere.

## Lighting:
### Warm, Ambient Lighting, Lanterns

Lighting in Bohemian interiors is warm and ambient, creating a cozy and inviting environment. Rather than using harsh overhead lighting, Boho decor often features a variety of light sources, including floor lamps, table lamps, string lights, and lanterns. Moroccan lanterns, with their intricate cut-out patterns, are a popular choice, casting beautiful shadows and adding to the room's exotic feel.

To enhance the layered lighting effect, consider incorporating candles and fairy lights. Candles, whether placed in decorative holders or arranged in groups, add a soft, flickering glow that enhances the cozy ambiance. Fairy lights can be draped over furniture, wrapped around plants, or hung along walls to create a whimsical and enchanting atmosphere. This combination of different light sources at varying heights and intensities helps to create a multi-dimensional and inviting space, perfect for relaxation and social gatherings.

INSPIRATIONAL HOME DECOR

## Materials:
### Natural Materials, Textiles, Handcrafted Items

Natural materials play a crucial role in Bohemian decor. Wood, rattan, and wicker are commonly used in furniture and accessories, adding warmth and texture to the space. Textiles are also a key component, with an emphasis on handcrafted items like macramé wall hangings, woven baskets, and hand-knotted rugs. These materials and items bring a sense of authenticity and craftsmanship to the decor.

INSPIRATIONAL HOME DECOR

## Color Scheme:
### Muted and Earthy Palettes

The color palette in Bohemian decor can be muted and earthy, often featuring soft beiges, warm grays, and light browns, complemented by cream and muted golds. These colors can be introduced through textiles, such as rugs, pillows, and throws, as well as through painted furniture and artwork. The goal is to create a cozy and inviting environment that reflects a love for natural materials and a relaxed, eclectic lifestyle. This approach to Bohemian decor emphasizes a serene and harmonious aesthetic, perfect for creating a tranquil and welcoming home.

By focusing on these muted and earthy tones, the Bohemian style retains its eclectic charm while creating a calming and cohesive space that feels collected and curated over time.

INSPIRATIONAL HOME DECOR

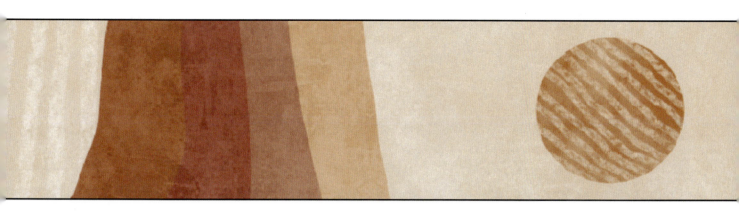

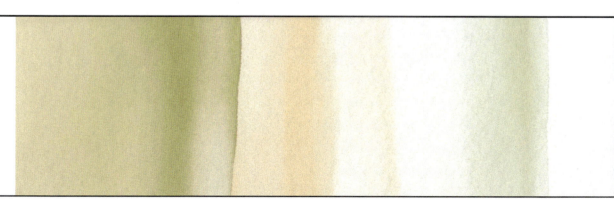

INSPIRATIONAL HOME DECOR

## Accessories:
### Art, Textiles, Personal Collections

Accessories in Bohemian decor are highly personal and often reflect the homeowner's travels and experiences. Walls are adorned with art, from traditional paintings to modern prints and everything in between. Textiles play a significant role, with layered rugs, throw blankets, and an abundance of cushions adding comfort and visual interest. Personal collections, such as vintage books, travel souvenirs, and unique finds from flea markets, add character and tell a story.

INSPIRATIONAL HOME DECOR

INSPIRATIONAL HOME DECOR

## Textures:
### Layered Textiles, Rugs, and Cushions

Layering is key in Bohemian decor, with a mix of textures creating a rich and inviting environment. Soft textiles like wool, cotton, and linen are used in abundance, from layered area rugs to throw blankets and cushions. This layering not only adds warmth and comfort but also creates a visually stimulating space. The key is to mix different textures to add depth and interest to the decor.

## Patterns:
### Mix of Patterns, Ethnic Prints

Patterns are a defining feature of Bohemian decor, with a mix of ethnic prints and bold designs creating a lively and eclectic look. Moroccan, Turkish, and Indian patterns are particularly popular, often seen in rugs, cushions, and wall hangings. The key to mastering Boho patterns is to mix and match without fear, creating a harmonious yet dynamic environment. Stripes, florals, and geometric patterns can all coexist beautifully in a Boho space.

INSPIRATIONAL HOME DECOR

### Plants:
### Abundant Greenery

Plants are a staple in Bohemian decor, bringing life and a touch of nature indoors. From large potted plants like fiddle leaf figs and monstera to hanging plants and small succulents, greenery is used to fill corners, adorn shelves, and add vibrancy to the space. Plants not only enhance the aesthetic but also contribute to a healthy and calming environment.

INSPIRATIONAL HOME DECOR

# Bohemian Decor Examples and Inspiration

INSPIRATIONAL HOME DECOR

INSPIRATIONAL HOME DECOR

INSPIRATIONAL HOME DECOR

INSPIRATIONAL HOME DECOR

INSPIRATIONAL HOME DECOR

INSPIRATIONAL HOME DECOR

"*Creativity is allowing yourself to make mistakes. Design is knowing which ones to keep.*"
**Scott Adams**

INSPIRATIONAL HOME DECOR

# Chapter 5: Industrial Style

INSPIRATIONAL HOME DECOR

# The Raw Appeal of Industrial Home Decor

Industrial home decor has its roots in the early 20th century, emerging from the practical and utilitarian design of industrial spaces and factories. These environments were characterized by their exposed architectural elements, such as brick walls, steel beams, and concrete floors, which were initially a byproduct of function over form. The Industrial Revolution played a significant role in shaping this aesthetic, as factories were designed to maximize efficiency and productivity with minimal concern for decoration or comfort.

In the mid-20th century, artists and creatives began repurposing these industrial spaces as living and working environments, particularly in urban areas where old factories and warehouses were being abandoned. This trend started in cities like New York and London, where loft apartments became popular among the artistic community. The raw, unfinished look of these spaces became a defining feature of the industrial style, celebrating the beauty in utility and the authenticity of exposed materials.

INSPIRATIONAL HOME DECOR

While the origins of industrial decor are firmly rooted in practicality, the style has evolved significantly over the years. The raw, unfinished aesthetic of old factories and warehouses has been refined and reimagined to suit modern living spaces. Today's industrial-style homes maintain the essence of the original aesthetic—exposed brick, steel, and concrete—but with a more polished and intentional approach.

Modern industrial decor often incorporates a mix of old and new elements. Vintage industrial furniture, such as metal stools and reclaimed wooden tables, is paired with contemporary pieces to create a balanced and cohesive look. High ceilings, open floor plans, and large windows are common features, enhancing the sense of space and light that is integral to the industrial style.

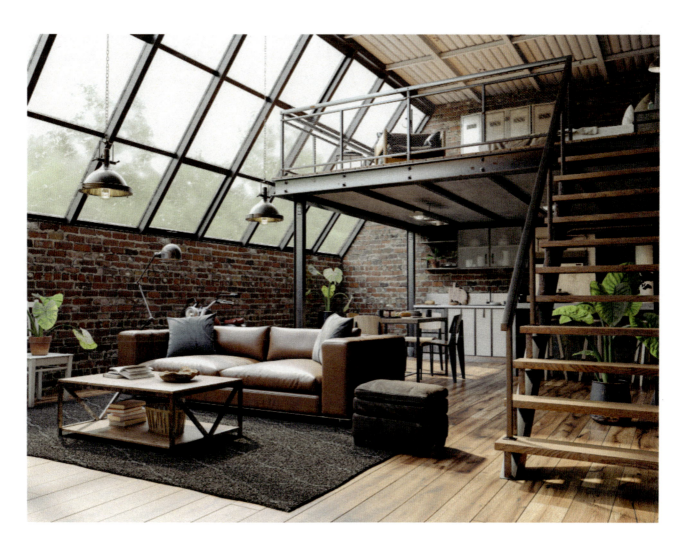

# Key Elements of Industrial Home Decor

**Furniture:**
Reclaimed and Repurposed Pieces, Metal and Wood Combinations

Furniture in industrial home decor often features reclaimed and repurposed pieces, giving a new life to items that have a history. This includes using materials like old factory carts, reclaimed wood, and vintage metal pieces. The combination of metal and wood is a defining characteristic, with items such as tables with metal frames and wooden tops, or metal chairs paired with wooden seats. This blend of materials highlights the utilitarian origins of the industrial style while adding warmth and character to the space.

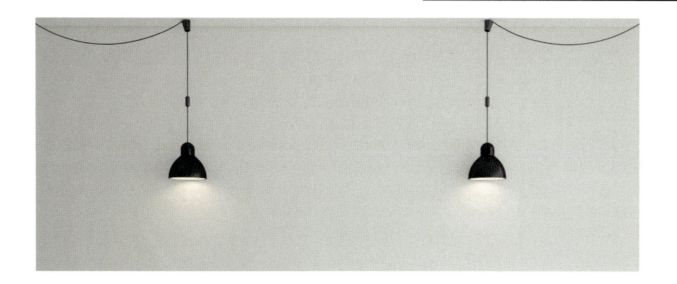

INSPIRATIONAL HOME DECOR

## Lighting:
### Industrial Fixtures, Exposed Bulbs

Lighting in industrial decor is both functional and decorative. Industrial fixtures often feature exposed bulbs, creating a raw and unpolished look. Pendant lights with metal shades, cage lights, and large floor lamps are common. These fixtures often have a vintage or salvaged appearance, with finishes like aged brass, blackened steel, or brushed nickel. The use of Edison bulbs, which have a warm, amber glow, adds to the industrial aesthetic by providing a nostalgic touch.

## Materials:
### Concrete, Steel, Brick

Industrial decor prominently features raw and rugged materials like concrete, steel, and brick. Concrete floors, steel beams, and exposed brick walls are quintessential elements that define the style. These materials emphasize durability and functionality, reflecting the industrial origins of the decor. Concrete can be polished for a sleek look or left rough for a more authentic feel. Steel is used in various forms, from structural elements to furniture and accessories, while exposed brick adds texture and warmth.

## Color Scheme:
### Monochromatic and Metallic Palettes

The color scheme in industrial home decor tends to be monochromatic and metallic. Neutral tones such as gray, black, and white dominate the palette, creating a clean and modern look. Metallic hues like steel gray, iron black, and copper are used to add depth and interest. Occasionally, accents of rich, earthy colors like rust, deep brown, and burnt orange are introduced through furniture and accessories to add warmth and contrast.

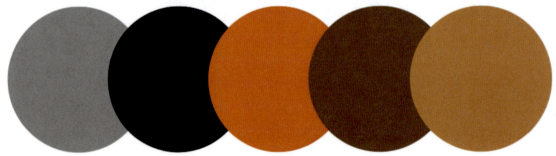

INSPIRATIONAL HOME DECOR

INSPIRATIONAL HOME DECOR

## Exposed Elements:
### Beams, Pipes, Ducts

One of the most distinctive features of industrial decor is the exposure of structural elements. Beams, pipes, and ducts are left visible, celebrating the architecture of the space. This not only adds visual interest but also pays homage to the industrial roots of the style. These elements are often painted in neutral or metallic colors to blend with the overall palette while standing out as design features.

## Textures:
### Rough, Raw Finishes

Textures play a crucial role in industrial decor, with an emphasis on rough and raw finishes. This includes exposed brick walls, distressed wooden surfaces, and unfinished metal elements. These textures create a sense of ruggedness and authenticity, reinforcing the industrial aesthetic. Soft furnishings like leather sofas, wool rugs, and linen cushions are used to balance the roughness with comfort and warmth.

## Detailing:
### Functional and Minimal Decor

Detailing in industrial decor is minimal and functional. The focus is on practicality and simplicity, with decor items serving a purpose beyond aesthetics. Shelving units made of metal and wood, simple storage solutions, and functional furniture pieces are typical. The minimal approach helps maintain the clean lines and open spaces characteristic of industrial style, ensuring that the decor is both practical and visually appealing.

## Accessories:
### Vintage Decor, Industrial Art

Accessories in industrial decor are carefully chosen to complement the overall aesthetic. Vintage decor items, such as old factory signs, industrial clocks, and reclaimed tools, add authenticity and a sense of history. Industrial art, including black-and-white photography, abstract metal sculptures, and factory-inspired artwork, enhances the decor. These accessories should be functional and minimal, avoiding clutter while adding character to the space.

# Industrial Decor Examples and Inspiration

INSPIRATIONAL HOME DECOR

INSPIRATIONAL HOME DECOR

INSPIRATIONAL HOME DECOR

INSPIRATIONAL HOME DECOR

INSPIRATIONAL HOME DECOR

INSPIRATIONAL HOME DECOR

INSPIRATIONAL HOME DECOR

INSPIRATIONAL HOME DECOR

# Chapter 6: Minimalist Style

INSPIRATIONAL HOME DECOR

# The Beauty of Minimalist Home Decor

Minimalist home decor has its roots in the modernist movements of the early 20th century. Influenced by the Bauhaus school in Germany and the De Stijl movement in the Netherlands, minimalism emphasized the idea that form follows function. These movements promoted simplicity, the use of industrial materials, and the elimination of unnecessary ornamentation. Key figures like *Ludwig Mies van der Rohe* and *Walter Gropius* championed the principles of minimalism, advocating for designs that were both functional and aesthetically pleasing.

Patio of Villa Wolf, built in 1926 in Guben (now Gubin in Poland) for Erich and Elisabeth Wolf. The villa was destroyed in the aftermath of World War II, and there are joint German-Polish plans for its reconstruction.

Traditional minimalism focused on reducing elements to their essential forms, stripping away anything superfluous. This approach has evolved over time, blending with contemporary design principles to create spaces that are both functional and visually appealing. Modern minimalist interiors often incorporate clean lines, open spaces, and a neutral color palette. The evolution of minimalism has also embraced sustainable and eco-friendly materials, reflecting a growing awareness of environmental issues.

# *Key Elements of Minimalist Home Decor*

**Furniture:**
Simple, Functional Designs, Minimal Pieces

Furniture in minimalist decor is characterized by its simple and functional design. Pieces are often sleek and unadorned, focusing on clean lines and practical use. The goal is to have fewer pieces, each serving a specific purpose without adding unnecessary clutter. Multi-functional furniture, such as storage ottomans or modular sofas, is commonly used to maximize space.

INSPIRATIONAL HOME DECOR

## Lighting:
### Natural Light, Understated Fixtures

Natural light is a crucial element in minimalist decor, enhancing the sense of openness and space. Large windows without heavy treatments allow light to flood the interior. When artificial lighting is needed, fixtures are kept understated and simple. Recessed lighting, track lights, and minimalist pendant lamps are popular choices, ensuring the lighting complements the clean aesthetic of the space.

INSPIRATIONAL HOME DECOR

**Materials:**
Natural Materials, Smooth Surfaces

The use of natural materials is essential in minimalist decor. Wood, stone, and metal are commonly used, often in their natural states to highlight their inherent beauty. Smooth surfaces are preferred to maintain a clean and uncluttered look. This can include polished concrete floors, sleek wooden furniture, and unadorned stone countertops.

INSPIRATIONAL HOME DECOR

**Patterns:**

Subtle or No Patterns

Patterns in minimalist decor are kept subtle or avoided altogether. If patterns are used, they are typically simple and understated, such as fine lines or geometric shapes. The focus remains on maintaining a clean and harmonious aesthetic, ensuring that patterns do not overwhelm the space.

INSPIRATIONAL HOME DECOR

## Color Scheme:
### Monochromatic and Neutral Palettes

A monochromatic and neutral color palette is a hallmark of minimalist decor. Whites, grays, blacks, and earth tones dominate, creating a serene and cohesive environment. These colors are often used in varying shades and textures to add subtle depth and interest without overwhelming the senses.

INSPIRATIONAL HOME DECOR

INSPIRATIONAL HOME DECOR

## Accessories:
### Minimal and Purposeful Decor Items

Accessories in minimalist decor are kept to a minimum, with each item chosen for its purpose and aesthetic contribution. Decor items are often functional, such as a single piece of artwork, a simple vase, or a clock. The key is to avoid clutter and ensure that each accessory enhances the overall simplicity and harmony of the space. Textures in minimalist decor are smooth and clean, contributing to the uncluttered and serene atmosphere. This includes materials like polished wood, sleek metal, and smooth stone. Soft textiles, such as wool or linen throws and cushions, add warmth and comfort without disrupting the clean lines and simplicity of the decor.

INSPIRATIONAL HOME DECOR

INSPIRATIONAL HOME DECOR

## Space:
### Maximizing Space with Minimal Clutter

Maximizing space and minimizing clutter are central principles of minimalist decor. Open floor plans, built-in storage solutions, and multi-functional furniture help achieve this goal. The aim is to create a sense of openness and flow, where each element has a purpose and contributes to the overall harmony of the space.

INSPIRATIONAL HOME DECOR

# Minimalist Decor Examples and Inspiration

INSPIRATIONAL HOME DECOR

INSPIRATIONAL HOME DECOR

INSPIRATIONAL HOME DECOR

INSPIRATIONAL HOME DECOR

INSPIRATIONAL HOME DECOR

INSPIRATIONAL HOME DECOR

"If you want a golden rule that will fit everything, this is it: Have nothing in your houses that you do not know to be useful or believe to be beautiful."
William Morris

INSPIRATIONAL HOME DECOR

# Chapter 7: Rustic Style

INSPIRATIONAL HOME DECOR

# The Cozy Charm of Rustic Home Decor

Rustic home decor has its roots in the rural countryside and traditional farmhouses, where practicality and simplicity were paramount. This style emerged from a need to create warm, inviting, and functional living spaces using readily available materials. Early rustic interiors were characterized by their use of natural elements like wood, stone, and metals, which were often left in their raw, unfinished state. This gave rustic decor its distinctive rugged and organic look. Historically, rustic decor was also influenced by the log cabins of early American settlers and the charming cottages of European villages. These homes were built with a focus on durability and comfort, often featuring handcrafted furniture, exposed beams, and large hearths that served as the heart of the home. The rustic style celebrates the beauty of imperfections and the charm of handcrafted items, reflecting a connection to nature and a simpler way of life. While traditional rustic decor remains beloved for its timeless charm and cozy appeal, the style has evolved to incorporate modern elements, creating what is known as modern rustic or contemporary rustic decor.

INSPIRATIONAL HOME DECOR

This evolution blends the warmth and texture of traditional rustic style with the clean lines and simplicity of modern design.Modern rustic decor retains the key elements of traditional rustic style, such as natural materials and a warm color palette, but introduces sleeker furniture, minimalist decor, and open floor plans. This combination results in spaces that are both comfortable and stylish, offering the best of both worlds. For example, a modern rustic living room might feature a reclaimed wood coffee table paired with a contemporary sofa, or a kitchen with state-of-the-art appliances set against a backdrop of exposed brick and wooden beams.

The use of sustainable and eco-friendly materials has also become a significant aspect of modern rustic decor. Reclaimed wood, repurposed furniture, and energy-efficient lighting are commonly incorporated, reflecting a growing awareness of environmental issues. This approach not only enhances the aesthetic appeal of rustic interiors but also aligns with the values of sustainability and mindful living.

INSPIRATIONAL HOME DECOR

# Key Elements of Rustic Home Decor

**Furniture:**

Wooden Pieces, Handcrafted Items

Furniture in rustic home decor is primarily made from wood, often featuring handcrafted and artisanal qualities. The emphasis is on sturdy, well-crafted pieces that showcase the natural beauty of the wood. Reclaimed and distressed wood is popular, adding character and history to the furniture. Key pieces might include farmhouse tables, wooden bed frames, and handcrafted chairs, all of which contribute to a warm and inviting atmosphere.

INSPIRATIONAL HOME DECOR

## Lighting:
Warm Lighting, Vintage Fixtures

Lighting in rustic decor focuses on creating a warm and cozy ambiance. Vintage fixtures, such as wrought iron chandeliers, lantern-style lights, and Edison bulb pendants, are commonly used. These fixtures not only provide ample lighting but also serve as decorative elements that enhance the rustic charm. Soft, warm light is preferred to create a comfortable and inviting environment.

INSPIRATIONAL HOME DECOR

INSPIRATIONAL HOME DECOR

**Materials:**
Wood, Stone, Natural Fibers

Rustic decor heavily relies on natural materials. Wood and stone are the primary materials used in everything from flooring and walls to furniture and accessories. Natural fibers like wool, cotton, and jute are used in textiles such as rugs, blankets, and cushions. These materials add to the authenticity and warmth of the space, creating a connection to nature and a sense of groundedness.

## Color Scheme:
Earthy and Natural Palettes

The color palette in rustic home decor is dominated by earthy and natural tones. Colors like browns, greens, and beiges are prevalent, reflecting the hues found in nature. These colors create a calming and soothing environment, enhancing the cozy feel of the space. Occasionally, deeper tones like burgundy or navy may be introduced to add depth and contrast.

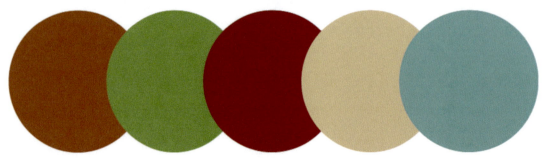

INSPIRATIONAL HOME DECOR

INSPIRATIONAL HOME DECOR

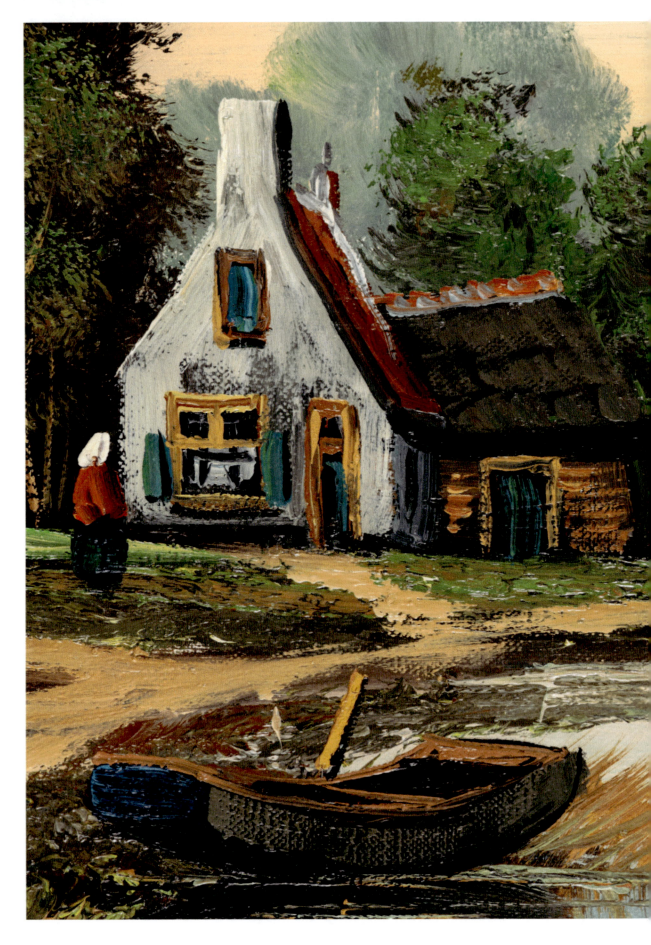

INSPIRATIONAL HOME DECOR

INSPIRATIONAL HOME DECOR

**Accessories:**
Rustic Decor, Antiques

Accessories play a significant role in rustic decor, with an emphasis on items that reflect a vintage or antique aesthetic. This includes things like old farm tools, vintage signs, pottery, and woven baskets. These accessories add character and a sense of history to the space. They are often displayed prominently, contributing to the overall rustic charm.

INSPIRATIONAL HOME DECOR

INSPIRATIONAL HOME DECOR

## Textures:
### Rough and Natural Textures

Textures in rustic decor are rich and varied, with a focus on rough and natural finishes. Exposed wooden beams, stone walls, and rough-hewn wooden furniture are common. Textiles like chunky knit blankets, woven rugs, and linen curtains add softness and contrast to the rougher elements, creating a balanced and inviting space.

## Patterns:
Plaids, Florals, Nature-Inspired

Patterns in rustic decor are inspired by nature and traditional designs. Plaid patterns, floral motifs, and other nature-inspired designs are commonly used in textiles such as curtains, cushions, and bedding. These patterns add visual interest and a touch of nostalgia, contributing to the cozy and welcoming atmosphere.

# Rustic Decor Examples and Inspiration

INSPIRATIONAL HOME DECOR

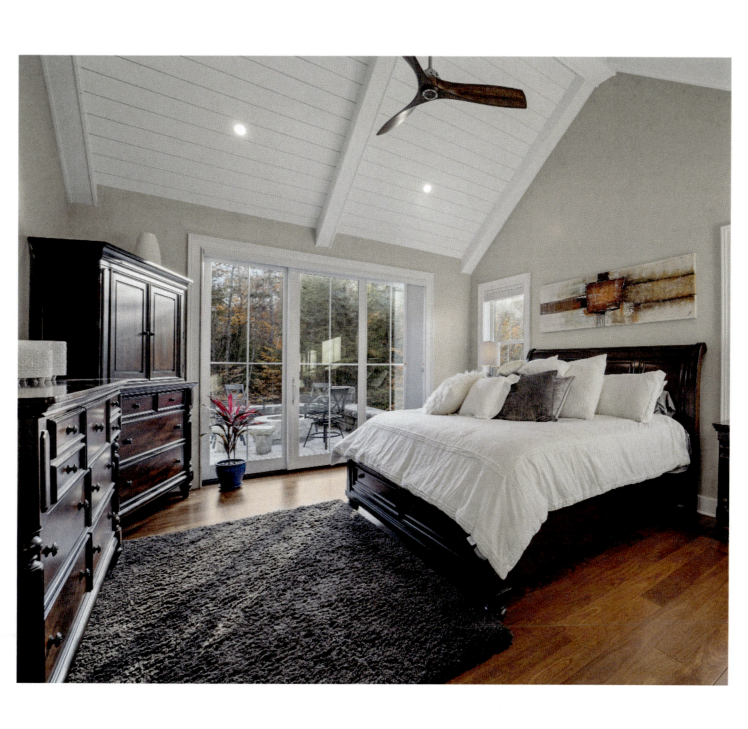

INSPIRATIONAL HOME DECOR

INSPIRATIONAL HOME DECOR

INSPIRATIONAL HOME DECOR

INSPIRATIONAL HOME DECOR

INSPIRATIONAL HOME DECOR

INSPIRATIONAL HOME DECOR

INSPIRATIONAL HOME DECOR

"Real comfort, visual and physical, is vital to every room."
Mark Hampton

INSPIRATIONAL HOME DECOR

# Chapter 8: Coastal Style

INSPIRATIONAL HOME DECOR

# The Breezy Comfort of Coastal Home Decor

Coastal home decor has its origins in the traditional homes found along the coastlines of the United States, particularly in New England, the Southern coasts, and beach towns along the West Coast. These homes were designed to reflect the natural beauty of their surroundings and to be practical for the seaside environment. Early coastal homes often featured light, airy spaces with large windows to take advantage of the ocean views and breezes. Materials were chosen for their durability against the salty air and humid conditions, leading to the use of weathered wood, wicker, and natural fibers.

The colors of the coastal decor were inspired by the sea and sky, with a palette dominated by shades of blue, white, and sandy neutrals. Nautical elements, such as rope, shells, and marine life motifs, were commonly incorporated into the decor. These homes were designed to be both comfortable and practical, providing a serene retreat from the harsh coastal weather.

Fort Lauderdale, USA – August 1, 2010

INSPIRATIONAL HOME DECOR

Over time, coastal home decor has evolved to incorporate modern design elements while retaining its connection to the seaside aesthetic. Modern coastal decor, often referred to as "beachy" or "contemporary coastal," maintains the light and airy feel of traditional coastal homes but with a more streamlined and sophisticated approach.

In modern coastal decor, the color palette has expanded to include more varied shades of blue, as well as greens and corals, reflecting the broader spectrum of seaside colors. White remains a dominant color, used to create a fresh and clean backdrop that enhances natural light and makes spaces feel larger and more open.

Materials have also evolved, with a mix of traditional and contemporary choices. Weathered wood and wicker are still popular, but they are often paired with sleek metals, glass, and polished finishes to create a more modern look. Textiles remain important, with an emphasis on natural fibers like cotton and linen, but modern prints and patterns, such as geometric designs and abstract ocean-inspired motifs, are now commonly used.

Modern coastal decor also incorporates more minimalist elements, with a focus on clean lines and uncluttered spaces. Furniture is often streamlined and functional, yet comfortable, designed to encourage relaxation and easy living. Decorative elements still draw inspiration from the sea, but they are used more sparingly and often in a more stylized form.

The evolution of coastal decor reflects a broader trend in interior design towards blending traditional and contemporary styles, creating spaces that are both timeless and current. This modern interpretation of coastal decor continues to celebrate the beauty of the seaside environment while adapting to the needs and tastes of contemporary living.

# Key Elements of Minimalist Home Decor

**Furniture:**

Light, Comfortable Pieces, Natural Materials

Furniture in coastal home decor is characterized by its light and comfortable nature. Pieces are typically made from natural materials such as wood, rattan, and wicker, which contribute to the airy and relaxed feel of the space. Sofas and chairs are often upholstered in light-colored fabrics, with slipcovers being a popular choice for their easy maintenance and casual elegance. The furniture layout is designed to promote relaxation and socializing, with plenty of seating options and an emphasis on comfort.

INSPIRATIONAL HOME DECOR

INSPIRATIONAL HOME DECOR

## Lighting:
## Natural Light, Breezy Fixtures

Natural light is a crucial component of coastal home decor, enhancing the bright and airy ambiance. Large windows, glass doors, and skylights are commonly used to maximize the influx of natural light. In addition to natural lighting, breezy light fixtures like pendant lights, chandeliers, and table lamps with light, airy shades are used to maintain a soft and welcoming glow. Fixtures made from materials such as rattan, bamboo, and linen complement the coastal aesthetic.

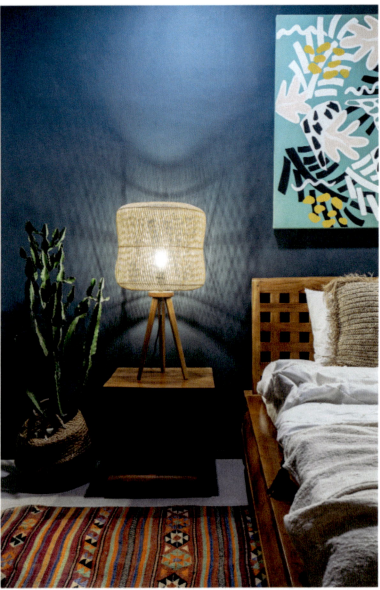

INSPIRATIONAL HOME DECOR

## Materials:
Wood, Rattan, Linen, and Jute

The use of natural materials is a hallmark of coastal decor. Wood, particularly in light or weathered finishes, is used extensively in furniture, flooring, and decorative accents. Rattan and wicker are popular choices for furniture and accessories, adding texture and a casual vibe. Textiles like linen and jute are used for curtains, rugs, and upholstery, contributing to the light and breezy feel of the space. These materials not only add to the aesthetic but also reflect the natural beauty of coastal environments.

INSPIRATIONAL HOME DECOR

INSPIRATIONAL HOME DECOR

**Color Scheme:**

Soft Blues, Whites, and Sandy Neutrals

The color palette in coastal home decor is inspired by the seaside, featuring soft blues, whites, and sandy neutrals. These colors create a serene and calming environment, reminiscent of the beach and ocean. Whites and neutrals are often used as the base colors to keep the space light and open, while blues and other coastal hues are introduced through accessories, textiles, and accent walls to add depth and interest.

INSPIRATIONAL HOME DECOR

INSPIRATIONAL HOME DECOR

INSPIRATIONAL HOME DECOR

INSPIRATIONAL HOME DECOR

## Accessories:
Nautical Decor, Beach-Themed Items

Accessories in coastal decor often include nautical and beach-themed items that enhance the seaside vibe. Common accessories include seashells, driftwood, coral, and nautical artifacts such as compasses, ship wheels, and lanterns. These items are often displayed in a way that feels collected and curated, adding character and a personal touch to the space. The goal is to evoke the feeling of being by the sea, even when indoors.

INSPIRATIONAL HOME DECOR

INSPIRATIONAL HOME DECOR

**Textures:**

Light, Breezy Fabrics, Natural Textures

Textures play a significant role in coastal decor, with an emphasis on light and breezy fabrics and natural textures. Linen, cotton, and jute are commonly used in textiles to create a relaxed and comfortable atmosphere. These materials are often layered to add depth and interest without overwhelming the space. The combination of soft textiles with rougher natural textures like driftwood and rattan adds a tactile element that enhances the overall aesthetic.

INSPIRATIONAL HOME DECOR

## Patterns:
### Stripes, Nautical Motifs

Patterns in coastal decor often include classic nautical motifs such as stripes, anchors, and seashells. Striped patterns, particularly in blue and white, are a staple of coastal design and can be found in everything from rugs and pillows to curtains and bedding. These patterns add a sense of continuity and connection to the sea, reinforcing the coastal theme. Other nautical motifs can be subtly incorporated into the decor through artwork, textiles, and accessories.

INSPIRATIONAL HOME DECOR

## Indoor-Outdoor Flow:
### Seamless Transition Between Indoor and Outdoor Spaces

One of the key elements of coastal home decor is the seamless transition between indoor and outdoor spaces. This is achieved through the use of large windows, sliding glass doors, and open floor plans that blur the boundaries between the inside and the outside. Outdoor living spaces are often designed to complement the interior decor, creating a cohesive look and feel. This indoor-outdoor flow encourages a lifestyle that embraces nature and the coastal environment, making the home feel more expansive and connected to its surroundings.

INSPIRATIONAL HOME DECOR

INSPIRATIONAL HOME DECOR

# Coastal Decor Examples and Inspiration

INSPIRATIONAL HOME DECOR

INSPIRATIONAL HOME DECOR

INSPIRATIONAL HOME DECOR

INSPIRATIONAL HOME DECOR

INSPIRATIONAL HOME DECOR

# Chapter 9: Retro Style

INSPIRATIONAL HOME DECOR

# The Nostalgic Charm of Retro Home Decor

Retro home decor draws its inspiration from the design trends and cultural influences of the mid-20th century, particularly the 1950s to the 1970s. This era was marked by significant changes in society, technology, and aesthetics, all of which contributed to the unique and vibrant style of retro decor.

The 1950s, often seen as the beginning of the retro era, brought about a sense of optimism and prosperity post-World War II. This period saw the rise of bold colors, playful patterns, and innovative materials such as plastics and laminates. The influence of futuristic designs, inspired by the space race and technological advancements, was also evident. Furniture designs by icons such as *Charles and Ray Eames, Eero Saarinen, and George Nelson* became emblematic of this era, showcasing sleek lines, organic forms, and functional elegance.

George Nelson & Associates for Miller Furniture Co., Desk Model 4658, Zeeland, MI 1946, with 'Anywhere' Lamp by Greta Von Nessen for Nessen Studio Inc., NY.

The 1960s continued this trend with an emphasis on bright, psychedelic colors and bold geometric patterns. This decade was heavily influenced by pop culture and the counterculture movement, leading to eclectic and expressive decor. The use of innovative materials and a mix of styles from different periods and regions created a distinctive and dynamic aesthetic.

The 1970s brought a shift towards more earthy tones and natural materials, reflecting the environmental movement of the time. Patterns became more elaborate, with floral and paisley designs becoming popular. The eclectic mix of styles continued, with influences from bohemian, disco, and even early punk cultures.

INSPIRATIONAL HOME DECOR

While the retro style remains rooted in its mid-20th century origins, it has evolved to incorporate contemporary elements, resulting in a blend of old and new. This evolution reflects changing tastes and advancements in design and technology while maintaining the nostalgic charm of classic retro decor.

Modern interpretations of retro decor often focus on key elements from the original style but update them for contemporary living. For example, the bold colors and patterns of the 1960s might be used more sparingly or combined with neutral tones to create a balanced and sophisticated look. Iconic furniture designs from the 1950s are often reproduced with modern materials and ergonomic improvements, making them more suitable for today's lifestyles.

Technological advancements have also influenced modern retro decor. Appliances and gadgets with retro aesthetics are now equipped with the latest technology, offering both style and functionality. This includes everything from vintage-style refrigerators and record players to modern lighting fixtures with a retro flair.

Moreover, the sustainability movement has led to a resurgence of interest in vintage and retro items. Many people now seek out authentic mid-century pieces or high-quality reproductions, appreciating their durability and timeless appeal. This has also encouraged a mix-and-match approach, where retro elements are combined with other design styles to create unique and personalized spaces.

In summary, retro home decor has a rich historical background rooted in mid-20th century design movements. Its evolution has led to a harmonious blend of classic and contemporary elements, allowing for a nostalgic yet modern aesthetic that continues to captivate and inspire.

# Key Elements of Retro Home Decor

### Furniture:
Iconic Designs, Curved Forms, and Vibrant Upholstery

Retro home decor is renowned for its iconic furniture designs, which often feature bold shapes and vibrant upholstery. Pieces from the mid-20th century, such as the Eames lounge chair, Saarinen's tulip chairs, and Nelson's marshmallow sofa, are celebrated for their innovative and stylish forms. These items typically have sleek lines, organic curves, and a playful aesthetic. Vibrant upholstery in colors like mustard yellow, teal, and burnt orange adds to the lively and dynamic feel of retro interiors.

INSPIRATIONAL HOME DECOR

INSPIRATIONAL HOME DECOR

## Lighting:
Eye-Catching Fixtures, Vintage-Inspired Lamps

Lighting plays a crucial role in retro decor, with an emphasis on eye-catching fixtures and vintage-inspired lamps. Popular choices include sputnik chandeliers, lava lamps, and globe pendant lights. These fixtures often feature bold designs and vibrant colors, adding a touch of whimsy and nostalgia to the space. The lighting not only serves a functional purpose but also acts as a statement piece that enhances the overall retro vibe.

INSPIRATIONAL HOME DECOR

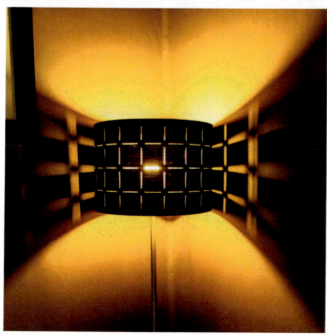

INSPIRATIONAL HOME DECOR

## Materials:
Plastics, Chromes, Woods, and Fabrics

A variety of materials are used in retro home decor, reflecting the innovative spirit of the mid-20th century. Plastics and chrome were revolutionary at the time and are frequently featured in furniture and accessories. These materials are often combined with natural elements like wood and fabrics to create a balanced and eclectic look. For example, a plastic Eames chair might be paired with a wooden table and upholstered in a bold fabric, showcasing the diverse materials that define retro style.

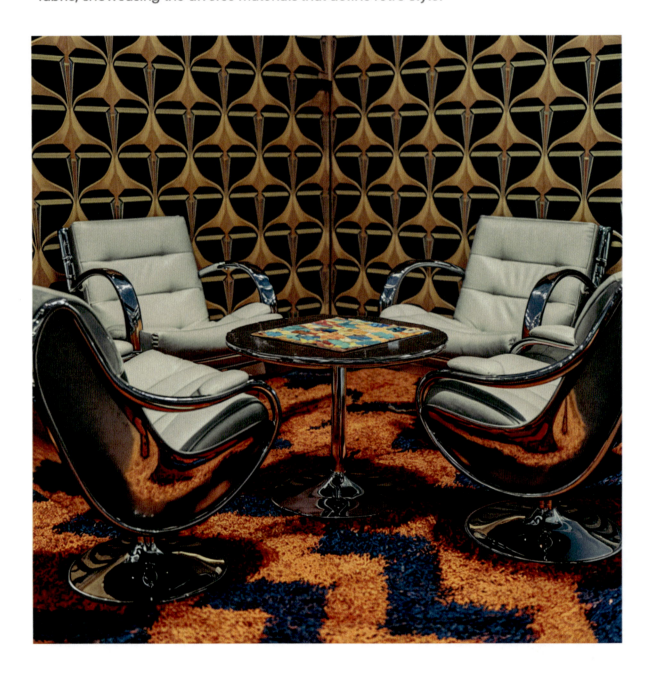

INSPIRATIONAL HOME DECOR

INSPIRATIONAL HOME DECOR

**Color Scheme:**
Dynamic and Energetic Palettes

Retro decor is characterized by its dynamic and energetic color palettes. Bright and bold colors such as teal, mustard yellow, avocado green, and hot pink are commonly used to create a lively and cheerful atmosphere. These vibrant hues are often paired with neutral tones like white, black, and gray to balance the overall look. The use of contrasting colors and striking combinations is a hallmark of retro design, making spaces feel vibrant and engaging.

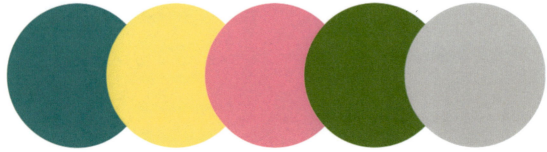

INSPIRATIONAL HOME DECOR

INSPIRATIONAL HOME DECOR

## Accessories:
Retro Accents, Pop Art, and Collectible Items

Accessories are essential in retro home decor, adding personality and character to the space. Retro accents such as rotary phones, vintage clocks, and mid-century art pieces are popular choices. Pop art, with its bold colors and graphic designs, is often featured on walls, paying homage to the cultural movements of the time. Collectible items like vinyl records, retro toys, and vintage posters add a nostalgic touch, creating a space that feels both personal and historical.

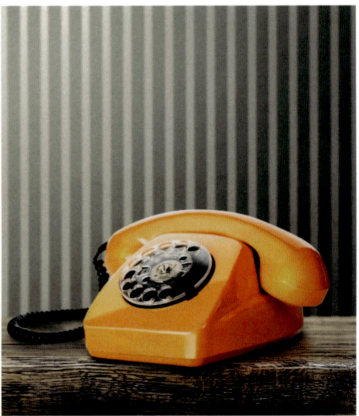

INSPIRATIONAL HOME DECOR

## Textures:
Smooth Plastics, Plush Fabrics, and Glossy Surfaces

Textures in retro decor are diverse and visually interesting. Smooth plastics, plush fabrics, and glossy surfaces are commonly used to add depth and contrast. For instance, a room might feature a glossy coffee table paired with a plush velvet sofa and smooth plastic chairs. The combination of different textures creates a tactile and dynamic environment, enhancing the retro aesthetic.

## Patterns:
Bold Geometrics, Florals, and Abstract Designs

Patterns play a significant role in retro decor, with bold geometrics, florals, and abstract designs being particularly popular. These patterns are often used in wallpapers, textiles, and rugs to add visual interest and energy to the space. Geometric patterns like chevrons, polka dots, and hexagons are common, as are floral prints in vibrant colors. Abstract designs inspired by the art and cultural movements of the time add a creative and eclectic touch.

## Nostalgic Elements:
### Celebrating Mid-Century Modern and Vintage Trends

Nostalgia is a key element of retro home decor, with a focus on celebrating mid-century modern and vintage trends. This includes incorporating iconic furniture pieces, vintage accessories, and classic patterns that evoke memories of the past. Retro decor often combines elements from different decades, creating a layered and eclectic look that feels both familiar and innovative. The use of nostalgic elements adds warmth and personality, making the space feel inviting and lived-in.

INSPIRATIONAL HOME DECOR

INSPIRATIONAL HOME DECOR

INSPIRATIONAL HOME DECOR

INSPIRATIONAL HOME DECOR

# Retro Decor Examples and Inspiration

INSPIRATIONAL HOME DECOR

INSPIRATIONAL HOME DECOR

INSPIRATIONAL HOME DECOR

INSPIRATIONAL HOME DECOR

INSPIRATIONAL HOME DECOR

INSPIRATIONAL HOME DECOR

# Chapter 10: Eclectic Style

# The Creative Freedom of Eclectic Home Decor

Eclectic home decor emerged from the desire to break away from the constraints of single-style design. Its roots can be traced back to the 19th century when architects and designers began to mix different styles and periods, influenced by the growing availability of global art and artifacts. This style gained momentum in the 20th century with the rise of global travel and the increasing availability of diverse cultural artifacts. The eclectic style is marked by its embrace of a wide range of influences, combining elements from different design movements such as Art Deco, Victorian, Mid-Century Modern, and Bohemian.

INSPIRATIONAL HOME DECOR

Traditional eclectic decor was characterized by a mix of styles and periods, often focusing on combining antique and vintage pieces with contemporary elements. Over time, this approach has evolved into modern eclectic decor, which still values diversity and individuality but often incorporates a more cohesive and curated look. Modern eclectic interiors might feature a mix of high-end designer pieces and thrift store finds, unified by a common color palette or theme. This evolution reflects a more refined approach to mixing styles, creating spaces that are both unique and harmonious.

INSPIRATIONAL HOME DECOR

# Key Elements of Eclectic Home Decor

### Furniture:
Mismatched Pieces, Vintage and Modern Mix

Eclectic home decor thrives on the combination of diverse furniture pieces, blending vintage and modern elements to create a unique and personalized space. This style encourages the use of mismatched chairs around a dining table, pairing a mid-century modern sofa with an antique coffee table, or incorporating a sleek, contemporary desk with a vintage bookshelf. The key is to maintain a sense of balance and harmony despite the variety of styles, ensuring that each piece contributes to the overall aesthetic.

INSPIRATIONAL HOME DECOR

## Lighting:
### Unique, Statement Fixtures

Lighting in eclectic decor is both functional and artistic. Statement fixtures such as ornate chandeliers, industrial pendant lights, and whimsical floor lamps are used to add character and drama to the space. These unique lighting pieces often serve as focal points, drawing attention and adding a layer of visual interest. The eclectic style allows for the mixing of different lighting types, from vintage-inspired sconces to modern LED fixtures, creating a well-lit and vibrant environment.

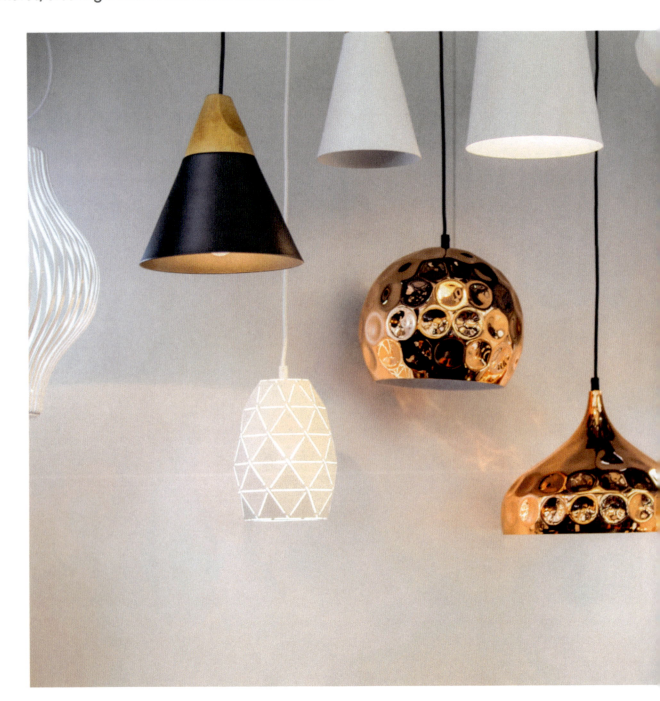

INSPIRATIONAL HOME DECOR

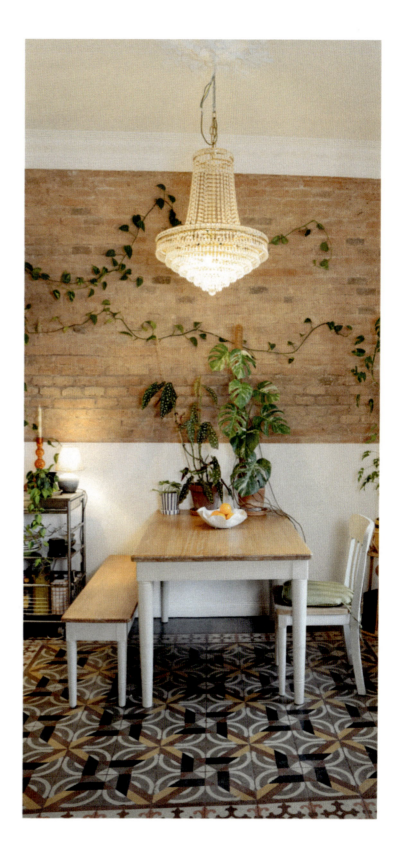

INSPIRATIONAL HOME DECOR

## Materials:
### Diverse Materials, Combining Old and New

The eclectic style embraces a mix of materials, combining old and new to create a rich and textured environment. Wood, metal, glass, and fabric are often used in various forms, from reclaimed wood tables and metal chairs to glass vases and textile wall hangings. This diversity in materials adds depth and complexity to the decor, allowing for creative expression and innovation. The juxtaposition of different textures and finishes, such as a rustic wooden bench next to a sleek marble countertop, exemplifies the eclectic approach to design.

INSPIRATIONAL HOME DECOR

## Color Scheme:
Bold, Diverse Palettes

Eclectic home decor is known for its bold and diverse color palettes. Unlike more restrained styles, eclectic decor often features vibrant hues and unexpected color combinations. Walls might be painted in rich, saturated colors like deep teal or mustard yellow, while furnishings and accessories bring in pops of contrasting colors. The use of patterned textiles and colorful artwork further enhances the dynamic and lively atmosphere. Despite the variety of colors, a sense of cohesion is maintained through the careful selection and placement of complementary shades.

INSPIRATIONAL HOME DECOR

INSPIRATIONAL HOME DECOR

INSPIRATIONAL HOME DECOR

INSPIRATIONAL HOME DECOR

## Accessories:
### Personalized Decor, Art, and Collections

Accessories play a crucial role in eclectic decor, providing opportunities to showcase personal style and interests. This includes a wide array of decor items, such as vintage finds, travel souvenirs, family heirlooms, and unique art pieces. Walls are often adorned with gallery-style displays of artwork, photographs, and eclectic wall hangings. Shelves and tables are filled with a mix of decorative objects, from quirky sculptures to antique trinkets. These personalized touches make the space feel lived-in and meaningful.

INSPIRATIONAL HOME DECOR

INSPIRATIONAL HOME DECOR

INSPIRATIONAL HOME DECOR

INSPIRATIONAL HOME DECOR

## Textures:
### Layered and Varied Textures

Layering different textures is essential in creating the rich and inviting feel of eclectic decor. This can include soft, plush rugs over hardwood floors, velvet cushions on leather sofas, and woven blankets draped over metal chairs. The mix of smooth, rough, shiny, and matte surfaces adds depth and interest, making the space feel dynamic and tactile. Textiles such as tapestries, throw pillows, and curtains in varied fabrics and patterns further enhance the layered look.

INSPIRATIONAL HOME DECOR

## Patterns:
### Mix of Patterns, from Florals to Geometrics

Patterns are a hallmark of eclectic decor, with a mix of florals, geometrics, stripes, and abstract designs often featured in textiles, wallpaper, and accessories. The key to successfully mixing patterns is to maintain a cohesive color scheme and balance bold designs with more subtle ones. For instance, a floral-patterned sofa might be paired with geometric throw pillows, while a striped rug anchors the room. This playful mix of patterns adds vibrancy and creativity to the space.

## Individuality:
### Reflecting Personal Style and Collections

The essence of eclectic decor lies in its celebration of individuality and personal expression. This style allows for the incorporation of unique collections, personal mementos, and favorite pieces from different eras and styles. The result is a space that feels deeply personal and reflective of the homeowner's tastes and experiences. Whether it's a collection of vintage cameras, a display of handmade pottery, or a gallery wall of family photos, these individual touches make the space truly one-of-a-kind.

INSPIRATIONAL HOME DECOR

# Eclectic Decor Examples and Inspiration

INSPIRATIONAL HOME DECOR

INSPIRATIONAL HOME DECOR

INSPIRATIONAL HOME DECOR

INSPIRATIONAL HOME DECOR

INSPIRATIONAL HOME DECOR

INSPIRATIONAL HOME DECOR

INSPIRATIONAL HOME DECOR

# A Heartfelt Farewell

As we conclude this journey through the diverse and inspiring world of home decor, we want to extend our heartfelt gratitude to everyone who has contributed to this book. Your support, insights, and encouragement have been invaluable.

Our goal with this book was to ignite creativity and offer practical guidance, helping you transform your living space with style and confidence. We hope the ideas and inspirations presented here have sparked your imagination and provided you with the tools to create a home that truly reflects your unique personality and taste.

If you found this book helpful, we would be incredibly grateful if **you could take a moment to leave a review**. Your feedback not only helps other readers discover this book but also inspires us to continue creating valuable content for you.

Thank you for being a part of this creative journey. We wish you all the best in your home decor endeavors.

With warm regards,

*Serene Art Press*

Made in the USA
Monee, IL
25 August 2024

b83f3c42-d176-458f-82e6-aa09b54bdc53R01